I0142059

St. Augustine of Hippo

A treatise concerning the
correction of the Donatists
[de correctione Donatistarum,
liber seu epistola CLXXXV.]
Circa a.d. 417.

[Early Church Fathers series]

This is a publication of:
New Apostolic Bible Covenant ®
"Nova Vulgate Foederis Apostolicam"
MMXII - MMXIX

ISBN: 978-0-244-77333-5
1st Edition April 2019
©2012-2019 Apostle Horn 'All rights reserved'
Book designer: Apostle Horn
Design cover and composition: Apostle Horn
Source cover photo: https://www.ancient-
origins.net/history-famous-people/saint-augustine-
hippo-and-his-detours-long-and-winding-path-
christianity-020654

Index:

Intro:

Saint Augustine of Hippo is one of the most important Christian theologians, and his works have exerted a great influence not only on the development of Western Christianity, but also on Western philosophy. Apart from the Roman Catholic Church, where he is honored as a saint as well as a Church Father, Saint Augustine of Hippo is also a prominent figure in the Anglican Communion, in the Eastern Orthodox Church, and even in some of the churches that grew out of the Protestant Reformation of the 16th century.

Augustine's youth:

Saint Augustine of Hippo was born on November 13, 354 AD, in Tagaste (now Souk Ahras, Algeria), a city then pertaining to Roman Africa. Though his family was not wealthy, they were highly respected in the city. His father was a man by the name of Patricius, and it is recorded that he was one of the curiales (leading members of a clan) of the city. Patricius was a pagan, though he converted to Christianity on his deathbed in accordance with his wife, Saint Monica's, wishes. Augustine too would be greatly influenced by the Christian virtues of his mother. As a boy, Augustine received a Christian education, and was enrolled amongst the catechumens (young Christians preparing for confirmation). Nevertheless, he only became a Christian later on in his life.

A treatise concerning the correction of the Donatists; Or Epistle CLXXXV.

A Letter of Augustin to Boniface, who, as we learn from Epistle 220, was Tribune, and afterwards Count in Africa. In it Augustin shows that the heresy of the Donatists has nothing in common with that of Arius; and points out the moderation with which it was possible to recall the heretics to the communion of the Church through awe of the imperial laws. He adds remarks concerning the savage conduct of the Donatists and Circumcelliones, concluding with a discussion of the unpardonable nature of the sin against the Holy Ghost.

Chapter 1

I must express my satisfaction, and congratulations, and admiration, my son Boniface, in that, amid all the cares of wars and arms, you are eagerly anxious to know concerning the things that are of God. From hence it is clear that in you it is actually a part of your military valor to serve in truth the faith which is in Christ. To place, therefore, briefly before your Grace the difference between the errors of the Arians and the Donatists, the Arians say that the Father, the Son, and the Holy Ghost are different in substance; whereas the Donatists do not say this, but acknowledge the unity of substance in the Trinity. And if some even of them have said that the Son was inferior to the Father, yet they have not denied that He is of the same substance; whilst the greater part of them declare that they hold entirely the same belief regarding the Father and the Son and the Holy Ghost as is held by the Catholic Church. Nor is this the actual question in dispute with them; but they carry on their unhappy strife solely on the question of communion, and in the perversity of their error maintain rebellious hostility against the unity of Christ. But sometimes, as we have heard, some of them, wishing to conciliate the Goths, since they see that they are not without a certain amount of power, profess to entertain the same belief as they. But they are refuted by the authority of their own leaders; for Donatus himself, of whose party they boast themselves to be, is never said to have held this belief. Let not, however, things like these disturb thee, my beloved son. For it is foretold to us that there must needs be heresies and stumbling-blocks, that we may be instructed among our enemies; and that so both our faith and our love may be the more approved, our faith, namely, that we should not be deceived by them; and our love, that we should take the utmost pains we can to correct the erring ones themselves; not only watching that they should do no injury to the weak, and that they should be delivered from their wicked error, but also praying for them, that God would open their understanding, and that they might comprehend the Scriptures. For in the sacred books, where the Lord Christ is made manifest, there is also His Church declared; but they, with wondrous blindness, while they would know nothing of Christ Himself save what is revealed in the Scriptures, yet form their notion of His Church from the vanity of human falsehood, instead of learning what it is on the authority of the sacred books. They recognize Christ together with us in that which is written, "They pierced my hands and my feet. They can tell all my bones: they look and stare upon me. They part my garments among them, and cast lots upon my vesture;" and yet they refuse to recognize the Church in that which follows shortly after: "All the ends of the world shall remember, and turn unto the Lord; and all the kindreds of the nations shall worship before Thee. For the kingdom is the Lord's; and He is the Governor among the nations." They recognize Christ together with us in that which is written, "The Lord hath said unto me,

Thou art my Son, this day have I begotten Thee;" and they will not recognize the Church in that which follows: "Ask of me, and I shall give Thee the heathen for Thine inheritance, and the uttermost parts of the earth for Thy possession." They recognize Christ together with us in that which the Lord Himself says in the gospel, "Thus it behoved Christ to suffer, and to rise from the dead the third day;" and they will not recognize the Church in that which follows: "And that repentance and remission of sins should be preached in His name among all nations, beginning at Jerusalem." And the testimonies in the sacred books are without number, all of which it has not been necessary for me to crowd together into this book. And in all of them, as the Lord Christ is made manifest, whether in accordance with His Godhead, in which He is equal to the Father, so that, "In the beginning was the Word, and; the Word was with God, and the Word was God;" or according to the humility of the flesh which He took upon Him, whereby "the Word was made flesh and dwelt among us;" so is His Church made manifest, not in Africa alone, as they most impudently venture in the madness of their vanity to assert, but spread abroad throughout the world. For they prefer to the testimonies of Holy Writ their own contentions, because, in the case of Cæcilianus, formerly a bishop of the Church of Carthage, against whom they brought charges which they were and are unable to substantiate, they separated themselves from the Catholic Church, that is, from the unity of all nations. Although, even if the charges had been true which were brought by them against Cæcilianus, and could at length be proved to us, yet, though we might pronounce an anathema upon him even in the grave, we are still bound not for the sake of any man to leave the Church, which rests for its foundation on divine witness, and is not the figment of litigious opinions, seeing that it is better to trust in the Lord than to put confidence in man. For we cannot allow that if Cæcilianus had erred, a supposition which I make without prejudice to his integrity, Christ should therefore have forfeited His inheritance. It is easy for a man to believe of his fellow-men either what is true or what is false; but it marks abandoned impudence to desire to condemn the communion of the whole world on account of charges alleged against a man, of which you cannot establish the truth in the face of the world. Whether Cæcilianus was ordained by men who had delivered up the sacred books, I do not know. I did not see it, I heard it only from his enemies. It is not declared to me in the law of God, or in the utterances of the prophets, or in the holy poetry of the Psalms, or in the writings of any one of Christ's apostles, or in the eloquence of Christ Himself. But the evidence of all the several scriptures with one accord proclaims the Church spread abroad throughout the world, with which the faction of Donatus does not hold communion. The law of God declared, "In thy seed shall all the nations of the earth be blessed." The Lord said by the mouth of His prophet, "From the rising of the sun, even unto the going down of the same, a pure sacrifice shall be offered unto my name: for my name shall be great among the heathen." The Lord said through the Psalmist, "He shall have dominion also from sea to sea, and from the river unto the ends of the earth." The Lord said by His apostle, "The gospel is come unto you, as it is in all the world, and bringeth forth fruit." The Son of God said with His own mouth, "Ye shall be witnesses unto me, both in Jerusalem, and in all Judea, and in Samaria, and even unto the uttermost part of the earth." Cæcilianus, the bishop of the Church of Carthage, is accused with the contentiousness of men; the Church of Christ, established among all nations, is recommended by the voice of God. Mere piety, truth, and love forbid us to receive against Cæcilianus the testimony of men whom we do not find in the Church, which has the testimony of God; for those who do not follow the testimony of God have forfeited the weight which otherwise would attach to their testimony as men.

Chapter 2

I would add, moreover, that they themselves, by making it the subject of an accusation, referred the case of Cæcilianus to the decision of the Emperor Constantine; and that, even after the bishops had pronounced their judgment, finding that they could not crush Cæcilianus, they brought him in person before the above-named emperor for trial, in the most determined spirit of persecution. And so they were themselves the first to do what they censure in us, in order that they may deceive the unlearned, saying that Christians ought not to demand any assistance from Christian emperors against the enemies of Christ. And this, too, they did not dare to deny in the conference which we held at the same time in Carthage: nay, they even venture to make it a matter of boasting that their fathers had laid a criminal indictment against Cæcilianus before the emperor; adding furthermore a lie, to the effect that they had there worsted him, and procured his condemnation. How then can they be otherwise than persecutors, seeing that when they persecuted Cæcilianus by their accusations, and were overcome by him, they sought to claim false glory for themselves by a most shameless life; not only considering it no reproach, but glorying in it as conducive to their praise, if they could prove that Cæcilianus had been condemned on the accusation of their fathers? But in regard to the manner in which they were overcome at every turn in the conference itself, seeing that the records are exceedingly voluminous, and it would be a serious matter to have them read to you while you are occupied in other matters that are essential to the peace of Rome, perhaps it may be possible to have a digest of them read to you, which I believe to be in the possession of my brother and fellow-bishop Optatus; or if he has not a copy, he might easily procure one from the church at Sitifa; for I can well believe that even that volume will prove wearisome enough to you from its lengthiness, amid the burden of your many cares. For the Donatists met with the same fate as the accusers of the holy Daniel. For as the lions were turned against them, so the laws by which they had proposed to crush an innocent victim were turned against the Donatists; save that, through the mercy of Christ, the laws which seemed to be opposed to them are in reality their truest friends; for through their operation many of them have been, and are daily being reformed, and return God thanks that they are reformed, and delivered from their ruinous madness. And those who used to hate are now filled with love; and now that they have recovered their right minds, they congratulate themselves that these most wholesome laws were brought to bear against them, with as much fervency as in their madness they detested them; and are filled with the same spirit of ardent love towards those who yet remain as ourselves, desiring that we should strive in like manner that those with whom they had been like to perish might be saved. For both the physician is irksome to the raging madman, and a father to his undisciplined son, the former because of the restraint, the latter because of the chastisement which he inflicts; yet both are acting in love. But if they were to neglect their charge, and allow them to perish, this mistaken kindness would more truly be accounted cruelty. For if the horse and mule, which have no understanding, resist with all the force of bites and kicks the efforts of the men who treat their wounds in order to cure them; and yet the men,

though they are often exposed to danger from their
teeth and heels, and sometimes meet with actual
hurt, nevertheless do not desert them till they restore
them to health through the pain and annoyance
which the healing process gives, how much more
should man refuse to desert his fellow-man, or
brother to desert his brother, lest he should perish
everlastingly, being himself now able to comprehend
the vastness of the boon accorded to himself in his
reformation, at the very time that he complained of
suffering persecution? As then the apostle says, "As
we have therefore opportunity, let us do good unto
all men, not being weary in well-doing," so let all be
called to salvation, let all be recalled from the path of
destruction, those who may, by the sermons of
Catholic preachers; those who may, by the edicts of
Catholic princes; some through those who obey the
warnings of God, some through those who obey the
emperor's commands. For, moreover, when
emperors enact bad laws on the side of falsehood, as
against the truth, those who hold a right faith are
approved, and, if they persevere, are crowned; but
when the emperors enact good laws on behalf of the
truth against falsehood, then those who rage against
them are put in fear, and those who understand are
reformed. Whosoever, therefore, refuses to obey the
laws of the emperors which are enacted against the
truth of God, wins for himself a great reward; but
whosoever refuses to obey the laws of the emperors
which are enacted in behalf of truth, wins for himself
great condemnation. For in the times, too, of the

prophets, the kings who, in dealing with the people of God, did not prohibit nor annul the ordinances which were issued contrary to God's commands, are all of them censured; and those who did prohibit and annul them are praised as deserving more than other men. And king Nebuchadnezzar, when he was a servant of idols, enacted an impious law that a certain idol should be worshipped; but those who refused to obey his impious command acted piously and faithfully. And the very same king, when converted by a miracle from God, enacted a pious and praiseworthy law on behalf of the truth, that every one who should speak anything amiss against the true God, the God of Shadrach, Meshach, and Abednego, should perish utterly, with all his house. If any persons disobeyed this law, and justly suffered the penalty imposed, they might have said what these men say, that they were righteous because they suffered persecution through the law enacted by the king: and this they certainly would have said, had they been as mad as these who make divisions between the members of Christ, and spurn the sacraments of Christ, and take credit for being persecuted, because they are prevented from doing such things by the laws which the emperors have passed to preserve the unity of Christ and boast falsely of their innocence, and seek from men the glory of martyrdom, which they cannot receive from our Lord. But true martyrs are such as those of whom the Lord says, "Blessed are they which are persecuted for righteousness' sake." It is not, therefore, those who suffer persecution for their unrighteousness, and for the divisions which they impiously introduce into Christian unity, but those who suffer for righteousness' sake, that are truly martyrs. For Hagar also suffered persecution at the hands of Sarah; and in that case she who persecuted was righteous, and she unrighteous who suffered persecution. Are we to compare with this persecution which Hagar suffered the case of holy David, who was persecuted by unrighteous Saul? Surely there is in essential difference, not in respect of his suffering, but because he suffered for righteousness' sake. And the Lord Himself was crucified with two thieves; but those who were joined in their suffering were separated by the difference of its cause. Accordingly, in the psalm, we must interpret of the true martyrs, who wish to be distinguished from false martyrs, the verse in which it is said, "Judge me, O Lord, and distinguish2 my cause from an ungodly nation." He does not say, Distinguish my punishment, but "Distinguish my cause." For the punishment of the impious may be the same; but the cause of the martyrs is always different. To whose mouth also the words are suitable, "They persecute me wrongfully; help Thou me;" in which the Psalmist claimed to have a right to be helped in righteousness, because his adversaries persecuted him wrongfully; for if they had been right in persecuting him, he would have deserved not help, but correction. But if they think that no one can be justified in using violence, as they said in the course of the conference that the true Church must necessarily be the one which suffers persecution, not the one inflicting it, in that case I no longer urge what I observed above; because, if the matter stand as they maintain that it does, then Cæcilianus must have belonged to the true Church, seeing that their fathers persecuted him, by pressing his accusation even to the tribunal of the emperor himself. For we maintain that he belonged to the true Church, not merely because he suffered persecution, but because he suffered it for righteousness' sake; but that they were alienated from the Church, not merely because they persecuted, but because they did so in unrighteousness. This, then, is our position. But if they make no inquiry into the causes for which each person inflicts persecution, or for which he suffers it, but think that it is a sufficient sign of a true Christian that he does not inflict persecution, but suffers it, then beyond all question they include Cæcilianus in that definition, who did not inflict, but suffered persecution; and they equally exclude their own fathers from the definition, for they inflicted, but did not suffer it. But this, I say, I forbear to urge. Yet one point I must press: If the true Church is the one which actually suffers persecution, not the one which inflicts it, let them ask the apostle of what Church Sarah was a type, when she inflicted persecution on her hand-maid. For he declares that the free mother of us all, the heavenly Jerusalem, that is to say, the true Church of God, was prefigured in that woman who cruelly entreated her hand-maid. But if we investigate the story further, we shall find that the handmaid rather persecuted Sarah by her haughtiness, than Sarah the handmaid by her severity: for the handmaid was doing wrong to her mistress; the mistress only imposed on her a proper discipline in her haughtiness. Again I ask, if good and holy men never inflict persecution upon any one, but only suffer it, whose words they think that those are in the psalm where we read, "I have pursued mine enemies, and overtaken them; neither did I turn again till they were consumed?" If, therefore, we wish either to declare or to recognize the truth, there is a persecution of unrighteousness, which the impious inflict upon the Church of Christ; and there is a righteous persecution, which the Church of Christ inflicts upon the impious. She therefore is blessed in suffering persecution for righteousness' sake; but they are miserable, suffering persecution for unrighteousness. Moreover, she persecutes in the spirit of love, they in the spirit of wrath; she that she may correct, they that they may overthrow: she that she may recall from error, they that they may drive headlong into error. Finally, she persecutes her enemies and arrests them, until they become weary in their vain opinions, so that they should make advance in the truth; but they, returning evil for good, because we take measures for their good, to secure their eternal salvation, endeavor even to strip us of our temporal safety, being so in love with murder, that they commit it on their own persons, when they cannot find victims in any others. For in proportion as the Christian charity of the Church endeavors to deliver them from that destruction, so that none of them should die, so their madness endeavors either to slay us, that they may feed the lust of their own cruelty, or even to kill themselves, that they may not seem to have lost the power of putting men to death.

Chapter 3

But those who are unacquainted with their habits think that they only kill themselves now that all the mass of the people are freed from the fearful madness of their usurped dominion, in virtue of the laws which have been passed for the preservation of unity. But those who know what they were accustomed to do before the passing of the laws, do not wonder at their deaths, but call to mind their character; and especially how vast crowds of them used to come in procession to the most frequented ceremonies of the pagans, while the worship of idols still continued, not with the view of breaking the idols, but that they might be put to death by those who worshipped them. For if they had sought to break the idols under the sanction of legitimate authority, they might, in case of anything happening to them, have had some shadow of a claim to be considered martyrs; but their only object in coming was, that while the idols remained uninjured, they themselves might meet with death. For it was the general custom of the strongest youths among the worshippers of idols, for each of them to offer in sacrifice to the idols themselves any victims that he might have slain. Some went so far as to offer themselves for slaughter to any travellers whom they met with arms, using violent threats that they would murder them if they failed to meet with death at their hands. Sometimes, too, they extorted with violence from any passing judge that they should be put to death by the executioners, or by the officer of his court. And hence we have a story, that a certain judge played a trick upon them, by ordering them to be bound and led away, as though for execution, and so escaped their violence, without injury to himself or them. Again, it was their daily sport to kill themselves, by throwing themselves over precipices, or into the water, or into the fire. For the devil taught them these three modes of suicide, so that, when they wished to die, and could not find any one whom they could terrify into slaying them with his sword, they threw themselves over the rocks, or committed themselves to the fire or the eddying pool. But who can be thought to have taught them this, having gained possession of their hearts, but he who actually suggested to our Saviour Himself as a duty sanctioned by the law, that He should throw Himself down from a pinnacle of the temple? And his suggestion they would surely have thrust far from them, had they carried Christ, as their Master, in their hearts. But since they have rather given place within them to the devil, they either perish like the herd of swine, whom the legion of devils drove down from the hill-side into the sea, or, being

®2012-2019 N.A.B.C.

rescued from that destruction, and gathered together in the loving bosom of our Catholic Mother, they are delivered just as the boy was delivered by our Lord, whom his father brought to be healed of the devil, saying that ofttimes he was wont to fall into the fire, and oft into the water. Whence it appears that great mercy is shown towards them, when by the force of those very imperial laws they are in the first instance rescued against their will from that sect in which, through the teaching of lying devils, they learned those evil doctrines, so that afterwards they might be made whole in the Catholic Church, becoming accustomed to the good teaching and example which they find in it. For many of the men whom we now admire in the unity of Christ, for the pious fervor of their faith, and for their charity, give thanks to God with great joy that they are no longer in that error which led them to mistake those evil things for good, which thanks they would not now be offering willingly, had they not first, even against their will, been severed from that impious association. And what are we to say of those who confess to us, as some do every day, that even in the olden days they had long been wishing to be Catholics; but they were living among men among whom those who wished to be Catholics could not be so through the infirmity of fear, seeing that if any one there said a single word in favor of the Catholic Church, he and his house were utterly destroyed at once? Who is mad enough to deny that it was right that assistance should have been given through the imperial decrees, that they

might be delivered from so great an evil, whilst those
whom they used to fear are compelled in turn to fear,
and are either themselves corrected through the
same terror, or, at any rate, whilst they pretend to be
corrected, they abstain from further persecution of
those who really are, to whom they formerly were
objects of continual dread? But if they have chosen to
destroy themselves, in order to prevent the
deliverance of those who had a right to be delivered,
and have sought in this way to alarm the pious
hearts of the deliverers, so that in their apprehension
that some few abandoned men might perish, they
should allow others to lose the opportunity of
deliverance from destruction, who were either
already unwilling to perish, or might have been
saved from it by the employment of compulsion;
what is in this case the function of Christian charity,
especially when we consider that those who utter
threats of their own violent and voluntary deaths are
very few in number in comparison with the nations
that are to be delivered? What then is the function of
brotherly love? Does it, because it fears the short
lived fires of the furnace for a few, therefore abandon
all to the eternal fires of hell? and does it leave so
many, who are either already desirous, or hereafter
are not strong enough to pass to life eternal, to perish
everlastingly, while taking precautions that some
few should not perish by their own hand, who are
only living to be a hindrance in the way of the
salvation of others, whom they will not permit to live
in accordance with the doctrines of Christ, in the

hopes that some day or other they may teach them too to hasten their death by their own hand, in the manner which now causes them themselves to be a terror to their neighbors, in accordance with the custom inculcated by their devilish tenets? or does it rather save all whom it can, even though those whom it cannot save should perish in their own infatuation? For it ardently desires that all should live, but it more especially labors that not all should die. But thanks be to the Lord, that both amongst us not indeed everywhere, but in the great majority of places and also in the other parts of Africa, the peace of the Catholic Church both has gained and is gaining ground, without any of these madmen being killed. But those deplorable deeds are done in places where there is an utterly furious and useless set of men, who were given to such deeds even in the days of old.

Chapter 4

And indeed, before those laws were put in force by the emperors of the Catholic faith, the doctrine of the peace and unity of Christ was beginning by degrees to gain ground, and men were coming over to it even from the faction of Donatus, in proportion as each learned more, and became more willing, and more master of his own actions; although, at the same time, among the Donatists herds of abandoned men were disturbing the peace of the innocent for one reason or another in the spirit of the most reckless madness. What master was there who was not compelled to live in dread of his own servant, if he had put himself under the guardianship of the Donatists? Who dared even threaten one who sought his ruin with punishment? Who dared to exact payment of a debt from one who consumed his stores, or from any debtor whatsoever, that sought their assistance or protection? Under the threat of beating, and burning, and immediate death, all documents compromising the worst of slaves were destroyed, that they might depart in freedom. Notes of hand that had been extracted from debtors were returned to them. Any one who had shown a contempt for their hard words were compelled by harder blows to do what they desired. The houses of innocent persons who had offended them were either razed to the ground or burned. Certain heads of families of honorable parentage, and brought up with a good education were carried away half dead after their deeds of violence, or bound to the mill, and compelled by blows to turn it round, after the fashion of the meanest beasts of burden. For what assistance from the laws rendered by the civil powers was ever of any avail against them? What official ever ventured so much as to breathe in their presence? What agents ever exacted payment of a debt which they had been unwilling to discharge? Who ever endeavored to avenge those who were put to death in their massacres? Except, indeed, that their own madness took revenge on them, when some, by provoking against themselves the swords of men, whom they obliged to kill them under fear of instant death, others by throwing themselves over sundry precipices, others by waters, others by fire, gave themselves over on the several occasions to a voluntary death, and gave up their lives as offerings to the dead by punishments inflicted with their own hands upon themselves. These deeds were looked upon with horror by many who were firmly rooted in the same superstitious heresy; and accordingly, when they supposed that it was sufficient to establish their innocence that they were ill contented with such conduct, it was urged against them by the Catholics: If these evil deeds do not pollute your innocence, how then do you maintain that the whole Christian world has been polluted by the alleged sin of Cæcilianus, which are either altogether calumnies, or at least not proved against him? How come you, by a deed of gross impiety, to separate yourselves from the unity of the Catholic Church, as from the threshing-floor of the Lord, which must needs contain, up to the time of the final winnowing, both corn which is to be stored in the garner, and chaff that is to be burned up with fire? And thus some were so convinced by argument as to come over to the unity of the Catholic Church, being prepared even to meet the hostility of abandoned men; whilst the greater number, though equally convinced, and though desirous to do the same, yet dared not make enemies of these men, who were so unbridled in their violence, seeing that some who had come over to us experienced the greatest cruelty at their hands. To this we may add, that in Carthage itself some of the bishops of the same party, making a schism among themselves, and dividing the party of Donatus among the lower orders of the Carthaginian people, ordained as bishop against bishop a certain deacon named Maximianus, who could not brook the control of his own diocesan. And as this displeased the greater part of them, they condemned the aforesaid Maximinus, with twelve others who had been present at his ordination, but gave the rest that were associated in the same schism a chance of returning to their communion on an appointed day. But afterwards some of these twelve, and certain others of those who had had the time of grace allowed to them, but had only returned after the day appointed, were received by them without degradation from their orders; and they did not venture to baptize a second time those whom the condemned ministers had baptized outside the pale of their communion. This action of theirs at once made strongly against them in favor of the Catholic party, so that their mouths were wholly closed. And on the matter being diligently spread abroad, as was only right, in order to cure men's souls of the evils of schism, and when it was shown in every possible direction by the sermons and discussions of the Catholic divines, that to maintain the peace of Donatus they had not only received back those whom they had condemned, with full recognition of their orders, but had even been afraid to declare that baptism to be void which had been administered outside their Church by men whom they had

condemned or even suspended; whilst, in violation
of the peace of Christ, they cast in the teeth of all the
world the stain conveyed by contact with some
sinners, it matters little with whom, and declared
baptism to be consequently void which had been
administered even in the very Churches whence the
gospel itself had come to Africa; seeing all this, very
many began to be confounded, and blushing before
what they saw to be mostly manifest truth, they
submitted to correction in greater numbers than was
their wont; and men began to breathe with a
somewhat freer sense of liberty from their cruelty,
and that to a considerably greater extent in every
direction. Then indeed they blazed forth with such
fury, and were so excited by the goadings of hatred,
that scarcely any churches of our communion could
be safe against their treachery and violence and most
undisguised robberies; scarcely any road secure by
which men could travel to preach the peace of the
Catholic Church in opposition to their madness, and
convict the rashness of their folly by the clear
enunciation of the truth. They went so far, besides, in
proposing hard terms of reconciliation, not only to
the laity or to any of the clergy, but even in a
measure to certain of the Catholic bishops. For the
only alternative offered was to hold their tongues
about the truth, or to endure their savage fury. But if
they did not speak about the truth, not only was it
impossible for any one to be delivered by their
silence, but many were even sure to be destroyed by
their submitting to be led astray; while if, by their

preaching the truth, the rage of the Donatists was again provoked to vent its madness, though some would be delivered, and those who were already on our side would be strengthened, yet the weak would again be deterred by fear from following the truth. When the Church, therefore, was reduced to these straits in its affliction, any one who thinks that anything was to be endured, rather than that the assistance of God, to be rendered through the agency of Christian emperors, should be sought, does not sufficiently observe that no good account could possibly be rendered for neglect of this precaution.

Chapter 5

But as to the argument of those men who are unwilling that their impious deeds should be checked by the enactment of righteous laws, when they say that the apostles never sought such measures from the kings of the earth, they do not consider the different character of that age, and that everything comes in its own season. For what emperor had as yet believed in Christ, so as to serve Him in the cause of piety by enacting laws against impiety, when as yet the declaration of the prophet was only in the course of its fulfillment, "Why do the heathen rage, and the people imagine a vain thing? The kings of the earth set themselves, and their rulers take counsel together, against the Lord, and against His Anointed;" and there was as yet no sign of that which is spoken a little later in the same psalm: "Be wise now, therefore, O ye kings; be instructed, ye judges of the earth. Serve the Lord with fear, and rejoice with trembling." How then are kings to serve the Lord with fear, except by preventing and chastising with religious severity all those acts which are done in opposition to the commandments of the Lord? For a man serves God in one way in that he is man, in another way in that he is also king. In that he is man, he serves Him by living faithfully; but in that he is also king, he serves Him by enforcing with suitable rigor such laws as ordain what is righteous, and punish what is the reverse. Even as Hezekiah served Him, by destroying the groves and the temples of the idols, and the high places which had been built in violation of the commandments of God; or even as Josiah served Him, by doing the same things in his turn; or as the king of the Ninevites served Him, by compelling all the men of his city to make satisfaction to the Lord; or as Darius served Him, by giving the idol into the power of Daniel to be broken, and by casting his enemies into the den of lions; or as Nebuchadnezzar served Him, of whom I have spoken before, by issuing a terrible law to prevent any of his subjects from blaspheming God. In this way, therefore, kings can serve the Lord, even in so far as they are kings, when they do in His service what they could not do were they not kings. Seeing, then, that the kings of the earth were not yet serving the Lord in the time of the apostles, but were still imagining vain things against the Lord and against His Anointed, that all might be fulfilled which was spoken by the prophets, it must be granted that at that time acts of impiety could not possibly be prevented by the laws, but were rather performed under their sanction. For the order of events was then so rolling on, that even the Jews were killing those who preached Christ, thinking that they did God service in so doing, just as Christ had foretold, and the heathen were raging against the Christians, and the patience of the martyrs was overcoming them all. But so soon as the fulfillment began of what is written in a later psalm, "All kings shall fall down before Him; all nations shall serve Him," what sober-minded man could say to the kings, "Let not any thought trouble you within your kingdom as to who restrains or attacks the Church of your Lord; deem it not a matter in which you should be concerned, which of your subjects may choose to be religious or sacrilegious," seeing that you cannot say to them, "Deem it no concern of yours which of your subjects may choose to be chaste, or which unchaste?" For why, when free-will is given by God to man, should adulteries be punished by the laws, and sacrilege allowed? Is it a lighter matter that a soul should not keep faith with God, than that a woman should be faithless to her husband? Or if those faults which are committed not in contempt but in ignorance of religious truth are to be visited with lighter punishment, are they therefore to be neglected altogether?

Chapter 6

It is indeed better (as no one ever could deny) that

men should be led to worship God by teaching, than that they should be driven to it by fear of punishment or pain; but it does not follow that because the former course produces the better men, therefore those who do not yield to it should be neglected. For many have found advantage (as we have proved, and are daily proving by actual experiment), in being first compelled by fear or pain, so that they might afterwards be influenced by teaching, or might follow out in act what they had already learned in word. Some, indeed, set before us the sentiments of a certain secular author, who said, "'Tis well, I ween, by shame the young to train, And dread of meanness, rather than by pain." This is unquestionably true. But while those are better who are guided aright by love, those are certainly more numerous who are corrected by fear. For, to answer these persons out of their own author, we find him saying in another place, "Unless by pain and suffering thou art taught, Thou canst not guide thyself aright in aught." But, moreover, holy Scripture has both said concerning the former better class, "There is no fear in love; but perfect love casteth out fear;" and also concerning the latter lower class, which furnishes the majority, "A servant will not be corrected by words; for though he understand, he will not answer." In saying, "He will not be corrected by words," he did not order him to be left to himself, but implied an admonition as to the means whereby he ought to be corrected; otherwise he would not have said, "He will not be corrected by words," but without any qualification, "He will not be corrected." For in another place he says that not only the servant, but also the undisdained son, must be corrected with stripes, and that with great fruits as the result; for he says, "Thou shall beat him with the rod, and shall deliver his soul from hell;" and elsewhere he says, "He that spareth the rod hateth his son." For, give us a man who with right faith and true understanding can say with all the energy of his heart, "My soul thirsteth for God, for the living God: when shall I come and appear before God?" And for such an one there is no need of the terror of hell, to say nothing of temporal punishments or imperial laws, seeing that with him it is so indispensable a blessing to cleave unto the Lord, that he not only dreads being parted from that happiness as a heavy punishment, but can scarcely even bear delay in its attainment. But yet, before the good sons can say they have "a desire to depart, and to be with Christ," many must first be recalled to their Lord by the stripes of temporal scourging, like evil slaves, and in some degree like good-for-nothing fugitives. For who can possibly love us more than Christ, who laid down His life for His sheep? And yet, after calling Peter and the other apostles by His words alone, when He came to summon Paul, who was before called Saul, subsequently the powerful builder of His Church, but originally its cruel persecutor, He not only constrained him with His voice, but even dashed him to the earth with His power; and that He might forcibly bring one who was raging amid the darkness of infidelity to desire the light of the heart, He first struck him with physical blindness of the eyes. If that punishment had not been inflicted, he would not afterwards have been healed by it; and since he had been wont to see nothing with his eyes open, if they had remained unharmed, the Scripture would not tell us that at the imposition of Ananias' hands, in order that their sight might be restored, there fell from them as it had been scales, by which the sight had been obscured. Where is what the Donatists were wont to cry: Man is at liberty to believe or not believe? Towards whom did Christ use violence? Whom did He compel? Here they have the Apostle Paul. Let them recognize in his case Christ first compelling, and afterwards teaching; first striking, and afterwards consoling. For it is wonderful how he who entered the service of the gospel in the first instance under the compulsion of bodily punishment, afterwards labored more in the gospel than all they who were called by word only; and he who was compelled by the greater influence of fear to love, displayed that perfect love which casts out fear. Why, therefore, should not the Church use force in compelling her lost sons to return, if the lost sons compelled others to their destruction? Although even men who have not been compelled, but only led astray, are received by their loving mother with more affection if they are recalled to her bosom through the enforcement of terrible but salutary laws, and are the objects of far more deep congratulation than those whom she had never lost.

Is it not a part of the care of the shepherd, when any
sheep have left the flock, even though not violently
forced away, but led astray by tender words and
coaxing blandishments, to bring them back to the
fold of his master when he has found them, by the
fear or even the pain of the whip, if they show
symptoms of resistance; especially since, if they
multiply with growing abundance among the
fugitive slaves and robbers, he has the more right in
that the mark of the master is recognized on them,
which is not outraged in those whom we receive but
do not rebaptize? For the wandering of the sheep is
to be corrected in such wise that the mark of the
Redeemer should not be destroyed on it. For even if
any one is marked with the royal stamp by a deserter
who is marked with it himself, and the two receive
forgiveness, and the one returns to his service, and
the other begins to be in the service in which he had
no part before, that mark is not effaced in either of
the two, but rather it is recognized in both of them,
and approved with the honor which is due to it
because it is the king's. Since then they cannot show
that the destination is bad to which they are
compelled, they maintain that they ought to be
compelled by force even to what is good. But we
have shown that Paul was compelled by Christ;
therefore the Church, in trying to compel the
Donatists, is following the example of her Lord,
though in the first instance she waited in the hopes of
needing to compel no one, that the prediction of the
prophet might be fulfilled concerning the faith of

kings and peoples. For in this sense also we may interpret without absurdity the declaration of the blessed Apostle Paul, when he says, "Having in a readiness to revenge all disobedience, when your obedience is fulfilled." Whence also the Lord Himself bids the guests in the first instance to be invited to His great supper, and afterwards compelled; for on His servants making answer to Him, "Lord, it is done as Thou hast commanded, and yet there is room," He said to them, "Go out into the highways and hedges, and compel them to come in." In those, therefore, who were first brought in with gentleness, the former obedience is fulfilled; but in those who were compelled, the disobedience is avenged. For what else is the meaning of "Compel them to come in," after it had previously said, "Bring in," and the answer had been made, "Lord, it is done as Thou commanded, and yet there is room?" If He had wished it to be understood that they were to be compelled by the terrifying force of miracles, many divine miracles were rather wrought in the sight of those who were first called, especially in the sight of the Jews, of whom it was said, "The Jews require a sign;" and, moreover, among the Gentiles themselves the gospel was so commended by miracles in the time of the apostles, that had these been the means by which they were ordered to be compelled, we might rather have had good grounds for supposing, as I said before, that it was the earlier guests who were compelled. Wherefore, if the power which the Church has received by divine appointment in its due season, through the religious character and the faith of kings, be the instrument by which those who are found in the highways and hedges that is, in heresies and schisms are compelled to come in, then let them not find fault with being compelled, but consider whether they be so compelled. The supper of the Lord is the unity of the body of Christ, not only in the sacrament of the altar, but also in the bond of peace. Of the Donatists themselves, indeed, we can say that they compel no man to any good thing; for whomsoever they compel, they compel to nothing else but evil.

Chapter 7

However, before those laws were sent into Africa by which men are compelled to come in to the sacred Supper, it seemed to certain of the brethren, of whom I was one, that although the madness of the Donatists was raging in every direction, yet we should not ask of the emperors to ordain that heresy should absolutely cease to be, by sanctioning a punishment to be inflicted on all who wished to live in it; but that they should rather content themselves with ordaining that those who either preached the Catholic truth with their voice, or established it by their study, should no longer be exposed to the furious violence of the heretics. And this they thought might in some measure be effected, if they would take the law which Theodosius, of pious memory, enacted generally against heretics of all kinds, to the effect that any heretical bishop or

clergyman, being found in any place, should be fined
ten pounds of gold, and confirm it in more express
terms against the Donatists, who denied that they
were heretics; but with such reservations, that the
fine should not be inflicted upon all of them, but only
in those districts where the Catholic Church suffered
any violence from their clergy, or from the
Circumcelliones, or at the hands of any of their
people; so that after a formal complaint had been
made by the Catholics who had suffered the
violence, the bishops or other ministers should
forthwith be obliged, under the commission given to
the officers, to pay the fine. For we thought that in
this way, if they were terrified and no longer dared
do anything of the sort, the Catholic truth might be
freely taught and held under such conditions, that
while no one was compelled to it, any one might
follow it who was anxious to do so without
intimidation, so that we might not have false and
pretended Catholics. And although a different view
was held by other brethren, who either were more
advanced in years, or had experience of many states
and places where we saw the true Catholic Church
firmly established, which had, however, been
planted and confirmed by God's great goodness at a
time when men were compelled to come in to the
Catholic communion by the laws of previous
emperors, yet we carried our point, to the effect that
the measure which I have described above should be
sought in preference from the emperors: it was
decreed in our council, and envoys were sent to the

court of the Count. But God in His great mercy, knowing how necessary was the terror inspired by these laws, and a kind of medicinal inconvenience for the cold and wicked hearts of many men, and for that hardness of heart which cannot be softened by words, but yet admits of softening through the agency of some little severity of discipline, brought it about that our envoys could not obtain what they had undertaken to ask. For our arrival had already been anticipated by the serious complaints of certain bishops from other districts, who had suffered much ill-treatment at the hands of the Donatists themselves, and had been thrust out from their sees; and, in particular, the attempt to murder Maximianus, the Catholic bishop of the Church of Bagai, under circumstances of incredible atrocity, had caused measures to be taken which left our deputation nothing to do. For a law had already been published, that the heresy of the Donatists, being of so savage a description that mercy towards it really involved greater cruelty than its very madness wrought, should for the future be prevented not only from being violent, but from existing with impunity at all; but yet no capital punishment was imposed upon it, that even in dealing with those who were unworthy, Christian gentleness might be observed, but a pecuniary fine was ordained, and sentence of exile was pronounced against their bishops or ministers. With regard to the aforesaid bishop of Bagai, in consequence of his claim being allowed in the ordinary courts, after each party had been heard

in turn, in a basilica of which the Donatists had taken
possession, as being the property of the Catholics,
they rushed upon him as he was standing at the
altar, with fearful violence and cruel fury, beat him
savagely with cudgels and weapons of every kind,
and at last with the very boards of the broken altar.
They also wounded him with a dagger in the groin
so severely, that the effusion of blood would have
soon put an end to his life, had not their further
cruelty proved of service for its preservation; for, as
they were dragging him along the ground thus
severely wounded, the dust forced into the spouting
vein stanched the blood, whose effusion was rapidly
on the way to cause his death. Then, when they had
at length abandoned him, some of our party tried to
carry him off with psalms; but his enemies, inflamed
with even greater rage, tore him from the hands of
those who were carrying him, inflicting grievous
punishment on the Catholics, whom they put to
flight, being far superior to them in numbers, and
easily inspiring terror by their violence. Finally, they
threw him into a certain elevated tower, thinking
that he was by this time dead, though in fact he still
breathed. Lighting then on a soft heap of earth, and
being espied by the light of a lamp by some men who
were passing by at night, he was recognized and
picked up, and being carried to a religious house, by
dint of great care, was restored in a few days from
his state of almost hopeless danger. Rumor, however,
had carried the tidings even across the sea that he
had been killed by the violence of the Donatists; and

when afterwards he himself went abroad, and was most unexpectedly seen to be alive, he showed, by the number, the severity, and the freshness of his wounds, how fully rumor had been justified in bringing tidings of his death. He sought assistance, therefore, from the Christian emperor, not so much with any desire of revenging himself, as with the view of defending the Church entrusted to his charge. And if he had omitted to do this, he would have deserved not to be praised for his forbearance, but to be blamed for negligence. For neither was the Apostle Paul taking precautions on behalf of his own transitory life, but for the Church of God when he caused the plot of those who had conspired to slay him to be made known to the Roman captain, the effect of which was that he was conducted by an escort of armed soldiers to the place where they proposed to send him, that he might escape the ambush of his foes. Nor did he for a moment hesitate to invoke the protection of the Roman laws, proclaiming that he was a Roman citizen, who at that time could not be scourged; and again, that he might not be delivered to the Jews who sought to kill him, he appealed to Cæsar, a Roman emperor, indeed, but not a Christian. And by this he showed sufficiently plainly what was afterwards to be the duty of the ministers of Christ, when in the midst of the dangers of the Church they found the emperors Christians. And hence therefore, it came about that a religious and pious emperor, when such matters were brought to his knowledge, thought it well, by the enactment of most pious laws, entirely to correct the error of this great impiety, and to bring those who bore the standards of Christ against the cause of Christ into the unity of the Catholic Church, even by terror and compulsion, rather than merely to take away their power of doing violence, and to leave them the freedom of going astray, and perishing in their error. Presently, when the laws themselves arrived in Africa, in the first place those who were already seeking an opportunity for doing so, or were afraid of the raging madness of the Donatists, or were previously deterred by a feeling of unwillingness to offend their friends, at once came over to the Church. Many, too, who were only restrained by the force of custom handed down in their homes from their parents, but had never before considered what was the groundwork of the heresy itself, had never, indeed, wished to investigate and contemplate its nature, beginning now to use their observation, and finding nothing in it that could compensate for such serious loss as they were called upon to suffer, became Catholics without any difficulty; for, having been made careless by security, they were now instructed by anxiety. But when all these had set the example, it was followed by many who were less qualified of themselves to understand what was the difference between the error of the Donatists and Catholic truth. Accordingly, when the great masses of the people had been received by the true mother with rejoicing into her bosom, there remained outside cruel crowds, persevering with unhappy animosity in that madness. Even of these the greater number communicated in feigned reconciliation, and others escaped notice from the scantiness of their numbers. But those who feigned conformity, becoming by degrees accustomed to our communion, and hearing the preaching of the truth, especially after the conference and disputation which took place between us and their bishops at Carthage, were to a great extent brought to a right belief. Yet in certain places, where a more obstinate and implacable body prevailed, whom the smaller number that entertained better views about communion with us could not resist, or where the masses were under the influence of a few more powerful leaders, whom they followed in a wrong direction, our difficulties continued somewhat longer. Of these places there are a few in which trouble still exists, in the course of which the Catholics, and especially the bishops and clergy, have suffered many terrible hardships, which it would take too long to go through in detail, seeing that some of them had their eyes put out, and one bishop his hands and tongue cut off, while some were actually murdered. I say nothing of massacres of the most cruel description, and robberies of houses, committed in nocturnal burglaries, with the burning not only of private houses, but even of churches, some being found abandoned enough to cast the sacred books into the flames. But we were consoled for the suffering inflicted on us by these evils, by the fruit which resulted from them. For

wherever such deeds were committed by
unbelievers, there Christian unity has advanced with
greater fervency and perfection, and the Lord is
praised with greater earnestness for having deigned
to grant that His servants might win their brethren
by their sufferings, and might gather together into
the peace of eternal salvation through His blood His
sheep who were dispersed abroad in deadly error.
The Lord is powerful and full of compassion, to
whom we daily pray that He will give repentance to
the rest as well, that they may recover themselves out
of the snare of the devil, by whom they are taken
captive at his will, though now they only seek
materials for calumniating us, and returning to us
evil for good; because they have not the knowledge
to make them understand what feelings and love we
continue to have towards them, and how we are
anxious, in accordance with the injunction of the
Lord, given to His pastors by the mouth of the
prophet Ezekiel, to bring again that which was
driven away, and to seek that which was lost.

Chapter 8

But they, as we have sometimes said before in other
places, do not charge themselves with what they do
to us; while, on the other hand, they charge us with
what they do to themselves. For which of our party is
there who would desire, I do not say that one of
them should perish, but should even lose any of his
possessions? But if the house of David could not
earn peace on any other terms except that Absalom

his son should have been slain in the war which he was waging against his father, although he had most carefully given strict injunctions to his followers that they should use their utmost endeavors to preserve him alive and safe, that his paternal affection might be able to pardon him on his repentance, what remained for him except to weep for the son that he had lost, and to console himself in his sorrow by reflecting on the acquisition of peace for his kingdom? The same, then, is the case with the Catholic Church, our mother; for when war is waged against her by men who are certainly different from sons, since it must be acknowledged that from the great tree, which by the spreading of its branches is extended over all the world, this little branch in Africa is broken off, whilst she is willing in her love to give them birth, that they may return to the root, without which they cannot have the true life, at the same time if she collects the remainder in so large a number by the loss of some, she soothes and cures the sorrow of her maternal heart by the thoughts of the deliverance of such mighty nations; especially when she considers that those who are lost perish by a death which they brought upon themselves, and not, like Absalom, by the fortune of war. And if you were to see the joy of those who are delivered in the peace of Christ, their crowded assemblies, their eager zeal, the gladsomeness with which they flock together, both to hear and sing hymns, and to be instructed in the word of God; the great grief with which many of them recall to mind their former error, the joy with which they come to the consideration of the truth which they have learned, with the indignation and detestation which they feel towards their lying teachers, now that they have found out what falsehoods they disseminated concerning our sacraments; and how many of them, moreover, acknowledge that they long ago desired to be Catholics, but dared not take the step in the midst of men of such violence, if, I say, you were to see the congregations of these nations delivered from such perdition, then you would say that it would have been the extreme of cruelty, if in the fear that certain desperate men, in number not to be compared with the multitudes of those who were rescued, might be burned in fires which they voluntarily kindled for themselves, these others had been left to be lost for ever, and to be tortured in fires which shall not be quenched. For if two men were dwelling together in one house, which we knew with absolute certainty to be upon the point of falling down, and they were unwillingly to believe us when we warned them of the danger, and persisted in remaining in the house; if it were in our power to rescue them, even against their will, and we were afterwards to show them the ruin threatening their house, so that they should not dare to return again within its reach, I think that if we abstained from doing it, we should well deserve the charge of cruelty. And further, if one of them should say to us, Since you have entered the house to save our lives, I shall forthwith kill myself; while the other was not indeed willing to come forth from the

house, nor to be rescued, but yet had not the
hardihood to kill himself: which alternative should
we choose, to leave both of them to be overwhelmed
in the ruin, or that, while one at any rate was
delivered by our merciful efforts, the other should
perish by no fault of ours, but rather by his own? No
one is so unhappy as not to find it easy enough to
deride what should be done in such a case. And I
have proposed the question of two individuals, one,
that is to say, who is lost, and one who is delivered;
what then must we think of the case where some few
are lost, and an innumerable multitude of nations are
delivered? For there are actually not so many
persons who thus perish of their own free will, as
there are estates, villages, streets, fortresses,
municipal towns, cities, that are delivered by the
laws under consideration from that fatal and eternal
destruction. But if we were to consider the matter
under discussion with yet greater care, I think that if
there were a large number of persons in the house
which was going to fall, and any single one of them
could be saved, and when we endeavored to effect
his rescue, the others were to kill themselves by
jumping out of the windows, we should console
ourselves in our grief for the loss of the rest by the
thoughts of the safety of the one; and we should not
allow all to perish without a single rescue, in the fear
lest the remainder should destroy themselves. What
then should we think of the work of mercy to which
we ought to apply ourselves, in order that men may
attain eternal life and escape eternal punishment, if

true reason and benevolence compel us to give such aid to men, in order to secure for them a safety which is not only temporal, but very short, for the brief space of their life on earth?

Chapter 9

As to the charge that they bring against us, that we covet and plunder their possessions, I would that they would become Catholics, and possess in peace and love with us, not only what they call theirs, but also what confessedly belongs to us. But they are so blinded with the desire of uttering calumnies, that they do not observe how inconsistent their statements are with one another. At any rate, they assert, and seem to make it a subject of most invidious complaint among themselves, that we constrain them to come in to our communion by the violent authority of the laws, which we certainly should not do by any means, if we wished to gain possession of their property. What avaricious man ever wished for another to share his possessions? Who that was inflamed with the desire of empire, or elated by the pride of its possession, ever wished to have a partner? Let them at any rate look on those very men who once belonged to them, but now are our brethren joined to us by the bond of fraternal affection, and see how they hold not only what they used to have, but also what was ours, which they did not have before; which yet, if we are living as poor in fellowship with poor, belongs to us and them alike; whilst, if we possess of our private means enough for our wants, it is no longer ours, inasmuch as we do not commit so infamous an act of usurpation as to claim for our own the property of the poor, for whom we are in some sense the trustees. Everything, therefore, that was held in the name of the churches of the party of Donatus, was ordered by the Christian emperors, in their pious laws, to pass to the Catholic Church, with the possession of the buildings themselves. Seeing, then, that there are with us poor members of those said churches who used to be maintained by these same paltry possessions, let them rather cease themselves to covet what belongs to others whilst they remain outside, and so let them enter within the bond of unity, that we may all alike administer, not only the property which they call their own, but also with it what is asserted to be ours. For it is written "All are yours; and ye are Christ's; and Christ is God's." Under Him as our Head, let us all be one in His one body; and in all such matters as you speak of, let us follow the example which is recorded in the Acts of the Apostles: "They were of one heart and of one soul: neither said any of them that aught of the things which he possessed was his own; but they had all things common." Let us love what we sing: "Behold, how good and how pleasant it is for brethren to dwell together in unity!" That so they may know, by their own experience, with what perfect truth their mother, the Catholic Church, calls out to them what the blessed apostle writes to the Corinthians: "I seek not yours, but you." But if we consider what is said in the Book of Wisdom,

"Therefore the righteous spoiled the ungodly;" and also what is said in the Proverbs, "The wealth of the sinner is laid up for the just;" then we shall see that the question is not, who are in possession of the property of the heretics? but who are in the society of the just? We know, indeed, that the Donatists arrogate to themselves such a store of justice, that they boast not only that they possess it, but that they also bestow it upon other men. For they say that any one whom they have baptized is justified by them, after which there is nothing left for them but to say to the person who is baptized by them that he must needs believe on him who has administered the sacrament; for why should he not do so, when the apostle says, "To him that believeth on Him that justifieth the ungodly, his faith is counted for righteousness?" Let him believe, therefore, upon the man by whom he is baptized, if it be none else that justifies him, that his faith may be counted for righteousness. But I think that even they themselves would look with horror on themselves, if they ventured for a moment to entertain such thoughts as these. For there is none that is just and able to justify, save God alone. But the same might be said of them that the apostle says of the Jews, that "being ignorant of God's righteousness, and going about to establish their own righteousness, they have not submitted themselves unto the righteousness of God." But far be it from us that any one of our number should call himself in such wise just, that he should either go about to establish his own righteousness, as though it were conferred upon him by himself, whereas it is said to him, "For what hast thou that thou didst not receive?" or venture to boast himself as being without sin in this world, as the Donatists themselves declared in our conference that they were members of a Church which has already neither spot nor wrinkle, nor any such thing, not knowing that this is only fulfilled in those individuals who depart out of this body immediately after baptism, or after the forgiveness of sins, for which we make petition in our prayers; but that for the Church, as a whole, the time will not come when it shall be altogether without spot or wrinkle, or any such thing, till the day when we shall hear the words, "O death, where is thy sting? O grave, where is thy victory? The sting of death is sin." But in this life, when the corruptible body presseth down the soul, if their Church is already of such a character as they maintain, they would not utter unto God the prayer which our Lord has taught us to employ: "Forgive us our debts." For since all sins have been remitted in baptism, why does the Church make this petition, if already, even in this life, it has neither spot nor wrinkle, nor any such thing? They would also have a fight to despise the warning of the Apostle John, when he cries out in his epistle, "If we say that we have no sin, we deceive ourselves, and the truth is not in us. But if we confess our sins, He is faithful and just to forgive us our sins, and to cleanse us from all unrighteousness." On account of this hope, the universal Church utters the petition, "Forgive us our debts," that when He sees

that we are not vainglorious, but ready to confess our
sins, He may cleanse us from all unrighteousness,
and that so the Lord Jesus Christ may show to
Himself in that day a glorious Church, not having
spot or wrinkle, or any such thing, which now He
cleanses with the washing of water in the word:
because, on the one hand, there is nothing that
remains behind in baptism to hinder the forgiveness
of every bygone sin (so long, that is, as baptism is not
received to no effect without the Church, but is either
administered within the Church, or, at least, if it has
been already administered without, the recipient
does not remain outside with it); and, on the other
hand, whatever pollution of sin, of whatsoever kind,
is contracted through the weakness of human nature
by those who live here after baptism, is cleansed
away in virtue of the same laver's efficacy. For
neither is it of any avail for one who has not been
baptized to say, "Forgive us our debts." Accordingly,
He so now cleanses His Church by the washing of
water in the word, that He may hereafter show it to
Himself as not having spot, or wrinkle, or any such
thing, altogether beautiful, that is to say, and in
absolute perfection, when death shall be "swallowed
up in victory." Now, therefore, in so far as the life is
flourishing within us that proceeds from our being
born of God, living by faith, so far we are righteous;
but in so far as we drag along with us the traces of
our mortal nature as derived from Adam, so far we
cannot be free from sin. For there is truth both in the
statement that "whosoever is born of God doth not

commit sin," and also in the former statement, that "if we say that we have no sin, we deceive ourselves, and the truth is not in us." The Lord Jesus, therefore, is both righteous and able to justify; but we are justified freely by no other grace than His. For there is nothing that justifieth save His body, which is the Church; and therefore, if the body of Christ bears off the spoils of the unrighteous, and the riches of the unrighteous are laid up in store as treasures for the body of Christ, the unrighteous ought not therefore to remain outside, but rather to enter within, that so they may be justified. Whence also we may be sure that what is written concerning the day of judgment, "Then shall the righteous man stand in great boldness before the face of such as have afflicted him, and made no account of his labors," is not to be taken in such a sense as that the Canaanite shall stand before the face of Israel, though Israel made no account of the labors of the Canaanite; but only as that Naboth shall stand before the face of Ahab, since Ahab made no account of the labors of Naboth, since the Canaanite was unrighteous, while Naboth was a righteous man. In the same way the heathen shall not stand before the face of the Christian, who made no account of his labors, when the temples of the idols were plundered and destroyed; but the Christian shall stand before the face of the heathen, who made no account of his labors, when the bodies of the martyrs were laid low in death. In the same way, therefore, the heretic shall not stand in the face of the Catholic, who made no account of his labors, when the laws of the Catholic emperors were put in force; but the Catholic shall stand in the face of the heretic, who made no account of his labors when the madness of the ungodly Circumcelliones was allowed to have its way. For the passage of Scripture decides the question in itself, seeing that it does not say, Then shall men stand, but "Then shall the righteous stand;" and they shall stand "in great boldness" because they stand in the power of a good conscience. But in this world no one is righteous by his own righteousness, that is, as though it were wrought by himself and for himself; but as the apostle says, "According as God hath dealt to every man the measure of faith." But then he goes on to add the following: "For as we have many members in one body, and all members have not the same office; so we, being many, are one body in Christ." And according to this doctrine, no one can be righteous so long as he is separated from the unity of this body. For in the same manner as if a limb be cut off from the body of a living man, it cannot any longer retain the spirit of life; so the man who is cut off from the body of Christ, who is righteous, can in no wise retain the spirit of righteousness, even if he retain the form of membership which he received when in the body. Let them therefore come into the framework of this body, and so possess their own labors, not through the lust of lordship, but through the godliness of using them aright. But we, as has been said before, cleanse our wills from the pollution of this concupiscence, even in the judgment of any enemy you please to name as judge, seeing that we use our utmost efforts in entreating the very men of whose labors we avail ourselves to enjoy with us, within the society of the Catholic Church, the fruits both of their labors and of our own.

Chapter 10

But this, they say, is the very thing which disquiets us, If we are unrighteous, wherefore do you seek our company? To which question we answer, We seek the company of you who are unrighteous, that you may not remain unrighteous; we seek for you who are lost, that we may rejoice over you as soon as you are found, saying, This our brother was dead, and is alive again; and was lost, and is found. Why, then, he says, do you not baptize me, that you might wash me from my sins? I reply: Because I do not do despite to the stamp of the monarch, when I correct the ill-doing of a deserter. Why, he says, do I not even do penance in your body? Nay truly, except you have done penance, you cannot be saved; for how shall you rejoice that you have been reformed, unless you first grieve that you had been astray? What, then, he says, do we receive with you, when we come over to your side? I answer, You do not indeed receive baptism, which was able to exist in you outside the framework of the body of Christ, although it could not profit you; but you receive the unity of the Spirit in the bond of peace without which no one can see God; and you receive charity, which, as it is written, "shall cover the multitude of sins." And in regard to this great blessing, without which we have the apostle's testimony that neither the tongues of men or of angels, nor the understanding of all mysteries, nor the gift of prophecy, nor faith so great as to be able to remove mountains, nor the bestowal of all one's goods to feed the poor, nor giving one's body to be burned, can profit anything; if, I say, you think this mighty blessing to be worthless or of trifling value, you are deservedly but miserably astray; and deservedly you must necessarily perish, unless you come over to Catholic unity. If, then, they say, it is necessary that we should repent of having been outside, and hostile to the Church, if we would gain salvation, how comes it that after the repentance which you exact from us we still continue to be clergy, or it may be even bishops in your body? This would not be the case, as indeed, in simple truth, we must confess it should not be the case, were it not that the evil is cured by the compensating power of peace itself. But let them give themselves this lesson, and most especially let those feel sorrow in their hearts, who are lying in this deep death of severance from the Church, that they may recover their life even by this sort of wound inflicted on our Catholic mother Church. For when the bough that has been cut off is grafted in, a new wound is made in the tree, to admit of its reception, that life may be given to the branch which was perishing for lack of the life that is furnished by the root. But when the newly-received branch has become identified with the stock in which it is received, the result is both vigor and fruit; but if they do not become identified, the engrafted bough withers, but the life of the tree continues unimpaired. For there is further a mode of grafting of such a kind, that without cutting away any branch that is within, the branch that is foreign to the tree is inserted, not indeed without a wound, but with the slightest possible wound inflicted on the tree. In like manner, then, when they come to the root which exists in the Catholic Church, without being deprived of any position which belongs to them as clergy or bishops after ever so deep repentance of their error, there is a kind of wound inflicted as it were upon the bark of the mother tree, breaking in upon the strictness of her discipline; but since neither he that planteth is anything, neither he that watereth, so soon as by prayers poured forth to the mercy of God peace is secured through the union of the engrafted boughs with the parent stock, charity then covers the multitude of sins. For although it was made an ordinance in the Church, that no one who had been called upon to do penance for any offense should be admired into holy orders, or return to or continue in the body of the clergy, this was done not to cause despair of any indulgence being granted, but merely to maintain a rigorous discipline; otherwise an argument will be raised against the keys that were given to the Church, of which we have the testimony of Scripture: "Whatsoever thou shall loose on earth shall be loosed in heaven." But lest it should so happen that, after the detection of offenses, a heart swelling with the hope of ecclesiastical preferment

might do penance in a spirit of pride, it was
determined, with great severity, that after doing
penance for any mortal sin, no one should be
admitted to the number of the clergy, in order that,
when all hope of temporal preferment was done
away, the medicine of humility might be endowed
with greater strength and truth. For even the holy
David did penance for deadly sin, and yet was not
degraded from his office. And we know that the
blessed Peter, after shedding the bitterest of tears,
repented that he had denied his Lord, and yet
remained an apostle. But we must not therefore be
induced to think that the care of those in later times
was in any way superfluous, who, when there was
no risk of endangering salvation, added something to
humiliation, in order that the salvation might be
more thoroughly protected, having, I suppose,
experienced a feigned repentance on the part of some
who were influenced by the desire of the power
attaching to office. For experience in many diseases
necessarily brings in the invention of many remedies.
But in cases of this kind, when, owing to the serious
ruptures of dissensions in the Church, it is no longer
a question of danger to this or that particular
individual, but whole nations are lying in ruin, it is
right to yield a little from our severity, that true
charity may give her aid in healing the more serious
evils. Let them therefore feel bitter grief for their
detestable error of the past, as Peter did for his fear
that led him into falsehood, and let them come to the
true Church of Christ, that is, to the Catholic Church

our mother; let them be in it clergy, let them be bishops unto its profit, as they have been hitherto in enmity against it. We feel no jealousy towards them, nay, we embrace them; we wish, we advise, we even compel those to come in whom we find in the highways and hedges, although we fail as yet in persuading some of them that we are seeking not their property, but themselves. The Apostle Peter, when he denied his Savior, and wept, and did not cease to be an apostle, had not as yet received the Holy Spirit that was promised; but much more have these men not received Him, when, being severed from the framework of the body, which is alone enlivened by the Holy Spirit, they have usurped the sacraments of the Church outside the Church and in hostility to the Church, and have fought against us in a kind of civil war, with our own arms and our own standards raised in opposition to us. Let them come; let peace be concluded in the virtue of Jerusalem, which virtue is Christian charity, to which holy city it is said, "Peace be in thy virtue, and plenteousness within thy palaces." Let them not exalt themselves against the solicitude of their mother, which she both has entertained and does entertain with the object of gathering within her bosom themselves, and all the mighty nations whom they are, or recently were, deceiving; at them not be puffed up with pride, that she receives them in such wise; let them not attribute to the evil of their own exaltation the good which she on her part does in order to make peace. So it has been her wont to come to the aid of multitudes who

were perishing through schisms and heresies. This
displeased Lucifer, when it was carried out in
receiving and healing those who had perished
beneath the poison of the Arian heresy; and, being
displeased at it, he fell into the darkness of schism,
losing the light of Christian charity. In accordance
with this principle the Church of Africa has
recognized the Donatists from the very beginning,
obeying herein the decree of the bishops who gave
sentence in the Church at Rome between Cæcilianus
and the party of Donatus; and having condemned
one bishop named Donatus, who was proved to have
been the author of the schism, they determined that
the others should be received, after correction, with
full recognition of their orders even if they had been
ordained outside the Church, not that they could
have the Holy Spirit even outside the unity of the
body of Christ, but, in the first place, for the sake of
those whom it was possible they might deceive while
they remained outside, and prevent from obtaining
that gift; and, secondly, that their own weakness also
being mercifully received within, might thus be
rendered capable of cure, no obstinacy any longer
standing in the way to close their eyes against the
evidence of truth. For what other intention could
have given rise to their own conduct, when they
received with full recognition of their orders the
followers of Maximianus, whom they had
condemned as guilty of sacrilegious schism, as their
council shows, and to fill whose places they had
already ordained other men, when they saw that the

people did not depart from their company, that all might not be involved in ruin? And on what other ground did they neither speak against nor question the validity of the baptism which had been administered outside by men whom they had condemned? Why, then, do they wonder, why do they complain, and make it the subject of their calumnies, that we receive them in such wise to promote the true peace of Christ, while yet they do not remember what they themselves have done to promote the false peace of Donatus, which is opposed to Christ? For if this act of theirs be borne in mind, and intelligently used in argument against them, they will have no answer whatsoever that they can make.

Chapter 11

But as to what they say, arguing as follows: If we have sinned against the Holy Ghost, in that we have treated your baptism with contempt, why is it that you seek us, seeing that we cannot possibly receive remission of this sin, as the Lord says, "Whosoever speaketh against the Holy Ghost, it shall not be forgiven him, neither in this world, neither in the world to come?" They do not perceive that according to their interpretation of the passage none can be delivered. For who is there that does not speak against the Holy Ghost and sin against him, whether we take the case of one who is not yet a Christian, or of one who shares in the heresy of Arius, or of Eunomius, or of Macedonius, who all say that He is a creature; or of Photinus, who denies that He has any substance at all, saying that there is only one God, the Father; or of any of the other heretics, whom it would now take too long a time to mention in detail? Are none, therefore, of these to be delivered? Or if the Jews themselves, against whom the Lord directed His reproach, were to believe in Him, would they not be allowed to be baptized? for the Saviour does not say, Shall be forgiven in baptism: but "Shall not be forgiven, neither in this world, neither in the world to come." Let them understand, therefore, that it is not every sin, but only some sin, against the Holy Ghost which is incapable of forgiveness. For just as when our Lord said, "If I had not come and spoken unto them, they had not had sin," it is clear that He did not wish it to be understood that they would have been free from all sin, since they were filled with many grievous sins, but that they would have been free from some special sin, the absence of which would have left them in a position to receive remission of all the sins which yet remained in them, viz., the sin of not believing in Him when He came to them; for they could not have had this sin, had He not come. In like manner, also, when He said, "Whosoever sinneth against the Holy Ghost,"or, "Whosoever speaketh against the Holy Ghost;" it is clear that He does not refer to every sin of whatsoever kind against the Holy Ghost, in word or deed, but would have us understand some special and peculiar sin. But this is the hardness of heart even to the end of this life, which leads a man to refuse to accept remission of his sins in the unity of the body of Christ, to which life is given by the Holy Ghost. For when He had said to His disciples "Receive the Holy Ghost," immediately added, Whosesoever sins ye remit, they are remitted unto them; and whosesoever sins ye retain, they are retained." Whosoever therefore has resisted or fought against this gift of the grace of God, or has been estranged from it in any way whatever to the end of this mortal life, shall not receive the remission of that sin, either in this world, or in the world to come, seeing that it is so great a sin that in it is included every sin; but it cannot be proved to have been committed by any one, till he has passed away from life. But so long as he lives here, "the goodness of God," as the apostle says, "is leading him to repentance;" but if he deliberately, with the utmost perseverance in iniquity, as the apostle adds in the succeeding verse, "after his hardness and impenitent heart, treasures up unto himself wrath against the day of wrath and revelation of the righteous judgment of God," he shall not receive forgiveness, neither in this world, neither in that which is to come. But those with whom we are arguing, or about whom we are arguing, are not to be despaired of, for they are yet in the body; but they cannot seek the Holy Spirit, except in the body of Christ, of which they possess the outward sign outside the Church, but they do not possess the actual reality itself within the Church of which that is the outward sign, and therefore they eat and drink damnation to themselves. For there is but one bread which is the sacrament of unity, seeing that, as the apostle says, "We, being many, are one bread, and one body." Furthermore, the Catholic Church alone is the body of Christ, of which He is the Head and Saviour of His body. Outside this body the Holy Spirit giveth life to no one seeing that, as the apostle says himself, "The love of God is shed abroad in our hearts by the Holy Ghost which is given unto us;" but he is not a partaker of the divine love who is the enemy of unity. Therefore they have not the Holy Ghost who are outside the Church; for it is written of them, "They separate themselves being sensual, having not the Spirit." But neither does he receive it who is insincerely in the Church, since this is also the intent of what is written: "For the Holy Spirit of discipline will flee deceit." If any one, therefore, wishes to receive the Holy Spirit, let him beware of continuing in alienation from the Church, let him beware of entering it in the spirit of dissimulation; or if he has already entered it in such wise, let him beware of persisting in such dissimulation, in order that he may truly and indeed become united with the tree of life. I have despatched to you a somewhat lengthy epistle, which may prove burdensome among your many occupations. If, therefore, it may be read to you even in portions, the Lord will grant you understanding, that you may have some answer which you can make for the correction and healing of those men who are commended to you as to a faithful son by our mother the Church, that you may correct and heal them, by the aid of the Lord wherever you can, and howsoever you can, either by speaking and replying to them in your own person, or by bringing them into communication with the doctors of the Church.